Gorillas

Patricia Kendell

HODDER
Wayland

An imprint of Hodder Children's Books

Alligators   Chimpanzees   Dolphins   Elephants
Gorillas   Grizzly Bears   Leopards   Lions
Pandas   Polar Bears   Sharks   Tigers

© 2002 White-Thomson Publishing Ltd

Produced for Hodder Wayland by White-Thomson Publishing Ltd

Editor: Kay Barnham
Designer: Tim Mayer
Consultant: Gezahegn Negussie - WWF Programme Officer,
  East Africa.
Language Consultant: Norah Granger, Senior Lecturer in Primary
  Education at the University of Brighton
Picture research: Shelley Noronha – Glass Onion Pictures

Published in Great Britain in 2002 by Hodder Wayland,
an imprint of Hodder Children's Books.

Photograph acknowledgements:
Bruce Coleman 1 & 18 (Mary Plage); FLPA 13 (Gerard Lacz),
23 (Silvestris); Images of Africa Photobank 14 (David Keith Jones);
Impact 11 (Yann Arthus Bertrand); NHPA 4 (Jeff Goodman),
27 & 28 (Martin Harvey), 9 (Minden Pictures); Oxford Scientific
Films 15 (Daniel Cox), 12, 17, 21 & 26 (Andrew Plumptre),
29 (Ian Redmond), 6, 7, 16, 19 & 20 (Konrad Wothe),
10 (Steve Turner); Still Pictures 25 (Mark Cawardine),
5 (Michel Gunther), 22 (Kevin Schafer), 24 (J C Vincent), 8.

British Library Cataloguing in Publication Data
Kendell, Patricia
  Gorilla. – (In the wild)
  1. Gorilla – Juvenile literature
  I. Title II. Barnham, Kay
  599.8'84

ISBN: 0 7502 4131 4

Printed in Hong Kong

Hodder Children's Books
A division of Hodder Headline Limited
338 Euston Road, London NW1 3BH

Produced in association with WWF-UK.
WWF-UK registered charity number 1081247.
A company limited by guarantee number 4016725.
Panda device © 1986 WWF ® WWF registered trademark owner.

Contents

Where gorillas live

Gorillas live in parts of Africa. Some live in the **tropical forests** of western and eastern Africa.

Other members of the gorilla family live in the misty mountain forests of central Africa. There are very few of these gorillas left in the wild.

Baby gorillas

A newly born gorilla is tiny and helpless.
The baby drinks milk from its mother.

Gorilla babies cling to their mother's chest, where they feel safe and warm. They do this until they are about 10 weeks old.

Looking after the babies

Gorilla mothers are very gentle and loving. They teach their babies which leaves and fruits are good to eat.

A baby gorilla will ride on its mother's back even after it learns to walk alone. It will do this until it is two and a half years old.

Family life

The babies live with their mothers in
a family group in their **home range**.
This group is led by a male **silverback**.

Gorillas are very friendly and live together peacefully.

Growing up

As the babies grow bigger they play games with one another. They practise the skills they will need when they grow up.

When this male gorilla is 12 years old, he will leave the group. Then he will find a **mate** and start a new family group of his own.

Finding food

Gorillas eat mainly bamboo shoots, fruits, leaves and roots. They sometimes travel long distances to find food.

In the mountain forests, there is often plenty of food. This means that these gorillas do not need to travel so far.

Eating

Gorillas sit down to eat. They reach out for leaves and fruit with their long arms. Sometimes they climb trees to find food, grasping the branches with their toes.

They pick stems, leaves and berries using their fingers and thumbs.

Rest and Sleep

After a good meal, the gorillas relax
for a few hours before feeding again.

As the sun goes down, each gorilla makes a nest of leafy stems. They sleep here until morning.

Keeping clean and warm

Gorillas like being together and helping each other to keep clean. They groom each other's fur to get rid of insects and dirt. This mother is cleaning her baby.

Mountain gorillas have thick fur that keeps them warm even in the cold rain.

Gentle Giants

Adult males are large and heavy.
They can look very fierce.

Silverbacks will stand and beat their chests if they are frightened. They will also warn the **troop** of danger. Gorillas do not fight much because they prefer a quiet life.

Threats...

Gorillas are in great danger. Their forest homes are being cut down because people want to use the land for farms.

Some people in Africa eat gorilla meat.
Park rangers try to stop this from happening.

25

...and dangers

These people are looking after a gorilla that has fallen into a trap.

Park rangers will try to find the family group
of an **orphan** baby. Sadly, some baby gorillas
are captured by **smugglers** and end up in zoos.

Helping gorillas to survive

Some people in Africa are working together to set up **protected areas** in the forest, where the gorillas can live safely. These park guides are watching the gorillas.

Local people can earn money from the tourists who come to see the gorillas. This means a better future for gorillas and people.

Further information

ORGANIZATIONS TO CONTACT

WWF-UK
Panda House, Weyside Park,
Godalming, Surrey GU7 1XR
Tel: 01483 426444
http://www.wwf.org.uk

International Primate Protection League
116 Judd Street,
London, WC1H 9NS
http://www.ippl.org

BOOKS

Apes (Endangered!): Casey Horton, Benchmark Books, 1996.

Gorillas: Seymour Simon, HarperCollins Children's Books, 2000.

Gorillas (Monkey Discovery Library): Lynn M Stone, Rourke Publishing Group, 1999.

Mountain Gorilla (Animals in Danger): Rod Theodorou, Heinemann, 2000.

Glossary

WEBSITES

Most young children will need adult help when visiting websites. Those listed have child-friendly pages to bookmark.

http://www.koko.org/kidsclub
This site features the story of Koko, a gorilla born in a zoo. There are interesting facts about gorillas and their natural habitat.

http://www.gorilla-haven.org/
A site that promotes education about gorilla conservation in the wild as well as in zoos. There are pages for children with stories about particular gorillas and links to other sites.

http://www.nationalgeographic.com/kids
Look here for fun facts, photographs and video sequences about mountain gorillas.

home range – the area where a gorilla troop lives and finds food.

mate – a female gorilla who a male gorilla has babies with.

orphan – an animal or person whose parents have both died.

park rangers – people who look after the special places where wild animals are protected.

protected areas – special places where wild animals are safe and free.

silverback – the name given to a male gorilla because of its silver-tipped fur.

smugglers – people who secretly take animals from the wild.

troop – a family group of gorillas.

tropical forests – forests in places where it is very hot and wet.

Index